How to Make Love
With Your Clothes On

101 Ways to Romance Your Husband

by

Dave and Anne Frahm

HONOR
BOOKS

How to Make Love With Your Clothes On
101 Ways to Romance Your Husband
ISBN 1-56292-349-8
Copyright © 1995 by Dave and Anne Frahm
P.O. Box 62130
Colorado Springs, CO 80962-2130

Published by Honor Books, Inc.
P.O. Box 55388
Tulsa, Oklahoma 74155

Presented To:

_____

Presented By:

_____

Date:

_____

Introduction

It took me twenty years of marriage to realize that my man needed romance. I thought romance was what men were expected to do for their women. You know, flowers and chocolates and holding the door open, and cards with sweet nothings scribbled inside. A step-up from the caveman's idea of clubbing her over the head and dragging her by the hair to his lair. (Is that when women started wearing short hair?)

I thought my husband's job was to do the romancing, and I would reciprocate by allowing him to watch the NBA play-offs unmolested. Was I wrong to think that my husband's only needs were a full belly, peace and quiet, and an occasional rendezvous under the covers. (Okay, okay, more than just occasional.)

But he needed romance? Lace and a subscription to *Victorian* magazine did not seem appropriate. Roses? Potpourri? Bubble bath? Help! I was in trouble. What was the key to romancing "the Stone"?

The answer came when we attended the wedding of a friend in Seattle. The pastor, when addressing the nearly-weds with sage words of wisdom, said the magic word. Pursuit! He said, "Don't give up pursuing each other." Had I taken my husband for granted? We all want to be pursued. It's the thrill of the chase!

How could I thrill my husband? To pursue him like when we were first dating. Webster's dictionary defines it this way: "to follow in order to capture." To chase him, and to capture his heart. But how?

So that weekend in Seattle, we wrote the bulk of this book. It became an adventure for my husband and me to dream of new, exciting ways to pursue each other. We knew that others like us had to be struggling with keeping the spark in their marriage. Especially when that spark can pay off in such a warm fire to cozy up to. . . .

*S*omeday after we have mastered the air, the winds, the tides, and gravity, we will harness for God the energies of love. And then for the second time in the history of the world, man will have discovered fire.

Teilhard de Chardin

1

Cuddle up next to him on the couch,
whispering provocative things
meant for his ears only.

*Warm breath
plus sweet nothings
equals hot blood.*

There is perhaps no better way to capture a man's heart, than for a woman to appreciate his sense of humor.

Laugh at his jokes.

Poetry ignites a flame,
music fans it.

3

Just before he gets home from work, put on his favorite "mood" music.

Sweet words,
respect and praise.
She sends him off,
to seize his days.
Sweet rewards,
a woman reaps.
His love she wants,
his love she keeps.

Make a list of all the things
you admire about him,
leaving it as a gift
next to his plate at breakfast.

While the kitchen is the "heart of the home," your bedroom is "home for the heart." Make it a place where intimacy and beauty abound.

5

Put your best decorating efforts
into your bedroom.

6

Take him to the local mall just to sit
and watch people go by.
Make up stories
about their lives: who they are,
what they do for a living, etc.

*Creativity and imagination are
the kissing cousins of romance.*

Give him a super deluxe
massage, complete with
flickering candles,
soft music,
and warm rubbing oil.

A man's preferences are what make him unique, make him interesting. Your interest in what he likes will make him feel respected and appreciated.

Ask him about his favorites:
colors, foods, movies, music,
things to do on Saturdays,
sports teams, etc....

Accolades before audiences
are care packages
for his heart.

While together
in the company of good friends,
brag about his latest accomplishment.

Catch his eye in a crowd
and wink at him.

It was just a wink.
Kind of a cute little blink.
But it began to make him think.

Put an ad in the local newspaper:

"Ten Things I Like Best
About My Husband"

Read poetry to him.

*Poetry is to the heart
what a match is to a candle.*

Who does not love true poetry,
He lacks a bosom friend
To walk with him,
And talk with him
And all his steps attend.
Who does not love true poetry—
Its rhythmic throb and swing
The treat of it
The sweet of it,
Along the paths of Spring.

Its joyous lilting melody
In every passing breeze,
The deep of it,
The sweep of it,
Through hours of toil or ease.
Its grandeur and sublimity—
Its majesty and might—
The feel of it,
The peal of it,
Through all the lonely night.

Its tenderness and soothing touch,
Like balm on evening air,
The feelingly
And healingly
Cures all the hurts of care.
Who does not love true poetry
Of sea and sky and sod—
The height of it
The might of it—
He has not known his God.

Henry Clay Hall, *Who Does Not Love True Poetry?*

Ideas:
In his left shoe,
under his pillow,
in his underwear drawer.

Write his parents
expressing your admiration
and respect for the son
they have raised.
Leave a copy for him
to stumble across.

*Honor bestowed
is an investment
with endless returns.*

Display his trophies,
certificates, and awards
where others can see them.

*There are naughty four-letter words.
"I told you so"
is a naughty four-word letter
addressed directly to his heart.
Anger and resentment
are its only reply.*

15

When he makes a mistake,
win points by refraining from saying,
"I told you so."

Write a poem about him,
framing it as a special gift.

Get out your wedding pictures
and look at them together.

The stroking of the male ego, combined with delighting his palate, are more than any man can resist. His heart will be in your hands.

18

In celebration
of a personal goal
he's achieved,
make him
his favorite meal.

Treasures,
kept and coddled by his wife,
make a man feel like
the woman he loves
enjoys the life
he has provided for her.

19

Keep a "memories chest."
Add items that represent
special events
in your life together.

*You're telling to him,
"I want the world to know
who you are and that
you are important."*

Have personal stationery
made for him with
his name imprinted on it.

21

Tell him he smells great.

22

Offer him
a cup of warm cocoa
before bed.

Half past nine—
high time for supper
"Cocoa love?"
"Of course my dear."
Helen thinks it quite delicious
John prefers it now to beer.
Knocking back the sepia potion,
Hubby winks, says, "Who's for bed?"

"Shan't be long," says Helen softly,
Cheeks a faintly flushing red.
For they've stumbled on the secret
of a love that never wanes
raft beneath the tumbled bedclothes,
cocoa coursing through their veins.

Stanley J. Sharpless, *In Praise of Cocoa, Cupid's Nightcap*

*There are pedestals
reserved in heaven
for wives with such an outlook.*

If he gets lost while driving,
win megapoints by saying,
"Hey, if we hadn't lost our way
we would never have seen
this part of the country."

24

Dedicate
a song to him
on the radio.

Read to him in bed
from interesting books.

26

Make it your aim
to be his biggest fan,
looking past his faults and faux pas
to see his talents and triumphs.

I think true love is never blind,

But rather brings an added light,

An inner vision quick to find

The beauties hid from common sight.

No soul can ever clearly see

Another's highest, noblest part;

Save through the sweet philosophy

And loving wisdom of the heart.

Your unanointed eyes shall fall
On him who fills my world with light;
You do not see my friend at all;
You see what hides him from your sight.
I see the feet that fain would climb;
You but the steps that turn astray;
I see the soul, unharmed, sublime;
You, but the garment and the clay.

You see a mortal, weak, misled,
Dwarfed ever by the earthly clod;
I see how manhood, perfected,
May reach the stature of a god.
Blinded I stood, as now you stand,
Till on mine eyes, with touches sweet,
Love, the deliverer, laid his hand,
And lo! I worship at his feet!

Phoebe Cary, *True Love*

27

Meet him at the door
wearing something soft and sexy.

28

Identify his interests
and buy him a subscription
to a related magazine.

Praise
for the work of his hands
goes deep
into the fabric of a man's soul.
He will not soon forget the woman
who has made his ego soar.

Praise
his latest "handy-man" project.

30

Admire his muscles.

At the next family gathering,
brag about his latest accomplishment.

Gather a smorgasbord of his favorite delights, placing them in a small box along with a note telling of your eager anticipation of his arrival home. Meet him at the door with a passionate kiss.

Pack a "love lunch" for him
to take with him to work.

Play "footsie" with him
while dining out together.

Ask for his advice
on an important decision.

Most men enjoy spectator sports.

To willingly join him is the action of a "goddess."

(Special note to all would-be "goddesses:"

Some men don't appreciate being asked

a lot of questions while caught up

in the heat of the competition.

Watch and learn, reserving questions for

commercials or time outs.)

35

If he's into sports,
let him enjoy watching.
In fact, join him.

36

Get him a card
from the friendship section
to show how
you cherish his friendship
above all others.

Identify the look he likes,
and take him out
on a clothing shopping spree
focused entirely upon him.

*There's nothing more compelling
to the human heart
than unconditional love
and acceptance.*

Tape a note
to the bathroom scale that says
"Perfect!"

39

Readily accept his apology
for forgetting an event
that was very important to you.

40

Ask him about his dreams.
"If time and money were of no issue,
what would you like to do?"

---

*Nothing reaches deeper
into the well of a man's heart
than the bucket that draws forth his dreams.*

---

*Women give beauty to the world.
Looking your best
is perceived by your husband
as your personal gift to him.*

M ake every effort
to look your best.

Take his side
if he finds himself upset
or in a dispute with someone else.

Ask him to help you
come to a conclusion
in an important matter.

A little thanks,
invested well,
pays huge dividends.

Identify and thank him for
the little things he's done
to make you feel wanted
and cherished.

45

Ask him
about things at work.

What does he like most about his job?
What would he change if he could?

46

If he travels away from home,
send along an assortment
of small gifts to be opened,
one each day,
while he's gone.

---

*Absence makes the heart grow fonder,
especially when gifts are involved.*

---

*The firm foundations
of a romantic relationship
are built
upon the delights
of surprise.*

To celebrate
one of his 364 "un-birthdays"
this year, bring him
breakfast in bed.

You'll be saying,
"I'm yours,
and I want everyone to know it."

Have glamour photos
made of you
for his office and wallet.

You'll be saying,
"What you do is important."

49

Buy him an especially comfortable desk chair for his office.

While mingling at a social gathering,
take his hand in yours
and give it a little squeeze—
one that says, "I'm yours."

51

Buy him one of those
VCR remotes that you
can program with your voice.

---

*Most men love gadgets,
especially the easy ones to use.
He'll love you for it.*

The sage advice is old but true.
Those who haven't heard are few.
If it's his heart that you pursue,
The quickest way is through
some food.

Plan a week's menu
of all his favorite foods.

Discovery
is a key element
woven into the fabric of romance.
Exploring the world together
opens the door
for greater discovery of each other.

53

Take him on
an exploration of nature
in his favorite park or woodlands.

Put a love note in his coat pocket.

For no other reason
than you want to,
surprise him with his favorite sweet.

Flowers
are a reflection in nature
of feminine beauty and sensitivity.
For a man to receive them
from a woman
means that she is sending
something of herself.

Arrange for flowers
to be delivered to his office.

Ideas:
A ride in a hot air balloon,
mountain biking in a state park,
go-carting at the local track,
attendance at a concert,
snorkeling in the ocean,
a boat ride on the river,
sight-seeing in an airplane, etc...

For his birthday,
arrange for a special adventure.

Listen in rapt attention
as he tells the tales
of his athletic accomplishments.

Buy him a classy attaché case
to carry his important papers.

*No woman has 'er conceived
more romantic notion than this,
Two lovers, a feast,
on a quilted spread,
lost in poetic bliss.*

Pack a picnic basket lunch
complete with
a variety of his favorite foods,
a blanket to sit on,
and a book of poetry to read to him.

61

For no other reason
than you want to,
buy him a beautiful new necktie.

Compliment him on his appearance.

This exercise has been known to spark unique insight into a person's sense of purpose, and help him see God's hand in his life. Your husband will appreciate your interest and willingness to listen.

63

Ask him this question:
"If you were to write a book about
your life, what would the title be?"

Ask him this question:
"Which would you choose and why—
being invisible, or being able to fly?"

*A question such as this
is a pathway to a man's
innermost dreams and fantasies.*

65

Arrange a special overnight
get-away at a local
Bed & Breakfast.
Pack a bag
for the both of you,
and surprise him.

*Of all the days that fill a year, this is the one that needs your greatest attention. For this is **his** day. A day to celebrate his existence. Treat it with utmost care!*

Put every effort
into planning out the details
of his next birthday celebration.

67

Rent a love story type movie
to watch together.

_Ideas: "Forever Young,"
"Always," "Sleepless in Seattle,"
"Much Ado About Nothing"_

Bring him a goblet
filled with white grape juice.
Let him take a sip,
then gently kiss his
moist lips for a taste.

*In Bible times
only a servant would touch
the feet of another.
Not only will massaging his feet
communicate your
commitment to serve him,
but it's also wonderfully relaxing.*

Give him a foot massage.

*Your unexpected
and provocative actions
will spark an immediate power
surge throughout his body.
Men love that kind of stuff.
You now have his complete attention.*

70

Next time you're alone
in an elevator together,
give him a big kiss on the lips
just before the door opens.

No dainty looking stuff,
for this hubby of the house.
He's a king in his castle;
a man, not a mouse.
So he needs a manly box
of tissues from his missy.
Something strong and hefty,
so he won't feel like a sissy.

71

Buy him manly looking
boxes of tissues.

*Surprise and creativity
spark the fires of romance.*

72

On each of seven
different slips of paper,
write a goodie you know he enjoys.
Let him pick one each day
as a special treat.

"Thank yous"
are food for the heart.

73

Call him during the day
just to tell him "thank you"
for something he's done
for you recently.

74

Turn your bedroom
into a romantic hide-away for dinner.
Flickering candle light,
alluring music,
and mouth-watering fare.

75

Wake him in the morning
with a kiss on the lips.

You *can give without loving,*
but you cannot love
without giving.

Amy Carmichael

76

Ask the simple question:
"What can I do for you today, honey?"

If he's a spiritually aware man, he will be exceedingly grateful. If he's not yet friends with God, this may open his heart.

Regularly ask him
about his concerns,
and keep a prayer journal
of things you're praying for him.

Leave an enticing message for him on his answering machine at work.

79

Buy him an easy chair
to be known from
that day forward as
"The Throne."

'Tis the human touch in this world that counts,

The touch of your hand and mine,

Which means far more to the fainting heart

Than shelter and bread and wine;

For shelter is gone when the night is o'er,

And bread lasts only a day,

But the touch of the hand

and the sound of the voice

Sing on in the soul alway.

Spencer Michael Free, *The Human Touch*

H old his hand
whenever you walk together.

81

Invite him on long,
leisurely walks
in the neighborhood.

Say, "I'm sorry"
even when you think you're right.

Sharing happy memories draws two hearts close. (Ideas: Family vacations, school days, adventures with friends, holiday celebrations, etc...)

Ask him about
his happiest
memories
as a child.

84

Turn down his side
of the bed covers,
leaving a chocolate
on the pillow.

Before bed,
offer him a scalp massage.

*Keeping him wondering
what you're going to do next
to express your love and affection
heightens interest and enthusiasm.*

Send him a singing telegram.

87

Put a love note
on the steering wheel
before he heads off to work.

88

Go fly a kite together.

*It has long been known
that dance
stirs the passions
in the human heart.*

When you hear a song you both like, ask him for this dance.

90

Take him out to the ball game.

*Ah, the roar of the popcorn
and the smell of the crowd!
He'll appreciate your
initiative in things he loves.*

91

Take him out
to the latest action/adventure movie
and share a tub of popcorn.

A personal pen
says to his world,
"I'm a man prepared to do business."
She that gave will be telling her man,
"I am proud to be your Mrs."

Buy him a fancy pen
with his name engraved upon it.

93

Spend several minutes
just kissing him lightly on the face,
eyelids, forehead, nose, and chin.

94

Pay to have top quality business cards designed and printed.

Regardless of his work,
a man's card is like a sword.
With it he leaves his mark on the world.
Your assistance in sharpening his armor
will be forever remembered and appreciated.

95

Take him out to a meal
at a dinner theater.

Sprinkle just a hint of your perfume
on his pillow.

Gloves and bats and shoes and more,
Find them all at the sporting goods store.
Men love games and competition,
Camping gear and ammunition.
So if you wish to please your man,
Make him happy, be his fan!
Then give this gift with a kiss to his face,
Sending him off to the sporting
goods place.

97

Set him loose in a
sporting goods store
with a gift certificate
and instructions
to buy something for himself.

98

Purchase a small, but quality, camera
for him to take with him
on business trips
so he can bring home pictures
of his travels to show you.

Read to him
from Song of Solomon in the Bible.

A spicy bit of biblical revelation
concerning the romantic love
between a husband and wife

A man's home is his castle.
His tools are his treasure!

After you use them,
always, but always,
put his tools back where they belong!

101

As a special gift,
make a collage of his life.
Include baby pictures.

---

*A heart deeply honored
is the fertile ground from which
romantic love blossoms.*